AMAZON FBA DECODED

How to Make an Extra $200 per Day Net Profit Selling Your Own Products on Amazon in 100 Days

By
Erdal Gul

Disclaimer

This document is geared towards providing exact and reliable information in regards to the topic and issue covered. The publication is sold with the idea that the publisher is not required to render accounting, officially permitted, or otherwise, qualified services. If advice is necessary, legal or professional, a practiced individual in the profession should be ordered.

- From a Declaration of Principles which was accepted and approved equally by a Committee of the American Bar Association and a Committee of Publishers and Associations.

The information provided herein is stated to be truthful and consistent, in that any liability, in terms of inattention or otherwise, by any usage or abuse of any policies, processes, or directions contained within is the solitary and utter responsibility of the recipient reader. Under no circumstances will any legal responsibility or blame be held against the publisher for any reparation, damages, or monetary loss due to the information herein, either directly or indirectly.

The information herein is offered for informational purposes only, and is universal as so. The presentation of the information is without contract or any type of guarantee assurance.

The trademarks that are used are without any consent, and the publication of the trademark is without permission or backing by the trademark owner. All trademarks and brands within this book are for clarifying purposes only and are owned by the owners themselves, not affiliated with this document.

Table of Contents

Introduction

Welcome to "Amazon FBA Decoded: How to Make an Extra $200 per Day Net Profit Selling Your Own Products on Amazon in 100 Days" in which you are going to learn how to leverage the Amazon FBA platform to your absolute advantage. I'll be taking you step by step through my proven strategies for success at launching your own private label business on FBA. By following the tips you find here and applying yourself you can get to the place where you are making $200 a day in *passive* income— income that essentially comes in on its own.

This is not something I claim lightly or can only verify secondhand. In fact, the Amazon FBA success story is *my own story*.I am not a millionaire and don't have influencers in my network. I am just a guy, just like you, sharing my experience in this book. I learned about Amazon FBA a year ago and have built it up into a business that grosses $15k a month, and with a profit margin of 40%, nets me $6K a month while working parttime. I'm also sharing lots of valuable content via my blog **OnlineSuccessDecoded.com**

In this book, I will walk you through everything I did to make that a reality. I did my due diligence and applied myself to finding the best product and positioning it ideally on Amazon, and you can do that too.

In "Amazon FBA Decoded: How to Make an Extra $200 per Day Net Profit Selling Your Own Products on Amazon in 100 Days" I will teach you:

- The ins and outs of Fulfillment by the Amazon platform
- The benefits of taking the FBA approach to private label business

- How to find the ideal product that is on the verge of becoming a top seller
- How to source reliable suppliers for your products
- The best ways to set up your product on Amazon
- How to brand your new company and give it a high profile on Amazon
- How to convert visitors to your product listing into buyers

This is also not an experience that is exclusive to readers in the U.S. who may be very familiar with Amazon. I'm living in Belgium and have built my business online just using my laptop. This business model is something that is a reality for anyone who can devote a bit of time upfront and has the initiative.

So, I hope you're ready! You are going to find out about one of the best opportunities out there right now. Within a few months, you could find yourself joining the thousands of people who are making a more than impressive living through passive income and FBA.

Let's get started.

Chapter One - What is Amazon FBA?

Fulfillment. It's a word with various meanings, but to those in product sales it means something pretty basic— fulfilling your customer's orders. What Amazon has done with their Fulfillment by Amazon program is create one of the most efficient and advanced fulfillment networks in the world. Amazon FBA gives you a centralized way in which to pack and ship products for your private label business. It also serves as a comprehensive CSM for handling customer service issues and inquiries.

How FBA Works

Amazon FBA delivers a number of services and advantages to a private label business. In short, we can summarize what Amazon FBA does for your business in the following way. Amazon FBA:

- Receives and stores your inventory of products
- Provides an e-commerce channel where customers can purchase your products
- Packs your products in Amazon-branded packaging
- Ships your products
- Provides customer support to your consumers

How this works is pretty simple. Let's walk through each component.

Amazon FBA Product Storage

As a private label business owner, you will source your own products to sell via Amazon FBA. Once you have selected these products— a process we will look at in detail later on in this book— you send your products to Amazon FBA's fulfillment centers.

Amazon FBA Inventory Management

Amazon FBA serves as a virtual inventory management system for your products. It receives and scans all of your inventory and provides you with an easy way to monitor that inventory through their online tracking system.

Amazon FBA E-Commerce

As you probably know, Amazon is a central hub for an enormous amount of e-commerce. Through Amazon FBA, you get a high-profile and centralized online marketplace for your goods. The stats speak for themselves— according to Amazon, FBA sellers have reported sales increases of 20% after joining FBA.There are just over 2 million sellers engaged in FBA right now and they account for nearly 40% of Amazon's total sales. It's an enormous and profitable enterprise and there is still plenty of room to grow.

Amazon FBA is also the ultimate customer service resource. Your customers can also combine what they order from you with other products purchased on Amazon, making it an appealing "one-stop" shop option for the busy modern consumer. Their high-speed picking and sorting system scans your inventory to locate products and even manages your order volume, allowing you to scale your business with ease as it grows.

Amazon FBA Shipment

Amazon FBA also takes care of all the packing and shipping of your goods to your customers. You get a good amount of flexibility, too— you can take advantage of Amazon discounted shipping or work with your own carrier. All shipments are tracked, and Amazon provides tracking information for all deliveries to your customers.

Amazon FBA Customer Service

Finally, FBA also serves as a CSM interface for your business, providing easy and responsive management of your customers' customer service needs.

FBA Fulfillment Fees

All of these services are covered by the FBA Fulfillment Fees Amazon charges for each product you sell. These fees are based on the size and nature of your product. These fees apply to products listed on Amazon.com, the U.S.-based Amazon site. Selling products via a different marketplace, such as Canada's Amazon.ca, may involve different fulfillment fees.

There are three main product categories that define the rate schedule for Amazon FBA fulfillment fees:

- Media
- Non-Media, and
- Oversize

Amazon also defines these fulfillment fees based on whether you are selling on Amazon.com alone or taking advantage of their Multi-Channel Fulfillment option. Multi-Channel Fulfillment allows your customers to purchase your Amazon-stored products via other sales channels and incurs higher fees.

The Amazon FBA Revenue Calculator

One of the major advantages of Amazon FBA is their Revenue

Calculator. This online interface gives you a way to assess fee costs as you establish your FBA business. By plugging in the fulfillment costs you would incur by taking care of fulfillment yourself, you get a real-time comparison between those costs and costs incurred if you go through Amazon FBA.

It's also an important tool because (as with any economy) the "prices" or fees on Amazon change on occasion. Pretty recently, in early 2015, Amazon adjusted their rates to reflect changing costs in fulfillment, transportation, and customer service. This affected their Pick & Pack and Weight Handling fees, as well as their Monthly Inventory Storage fees.

By using the Revenue Calculator, you can more effectively plan and make accommodations for these changes when they occur. So head over to the Revenue Calculator and play with it a bit. It's an invaluable tool as you start exploring the world of Amazon FBA.

URL: https://sellercentral.amazon.com/gp/fba/revenue-calculator/index.html/ref=ag_xx_cont_xx?ie=UTF8&lang=en_US

Fulfillment by Amazon Revenue Calculator

Provide your fulfillment costs and see real-time cost comparisons betwee

Disclaimer - This Fulfillment by Amazon Revenue Calculator should be used as a guide in evalua Revenue Calculator should be conducted to verify the results. Please consult the Amazon Service

Effective March 1, 2015, FBA's Monthly Inventory Storage Fees will be ch Fulfillment by Amazon Fee Changes.

→ Add your product name, UPC, EAN or ASIN (= i use the ASIN to calculate)

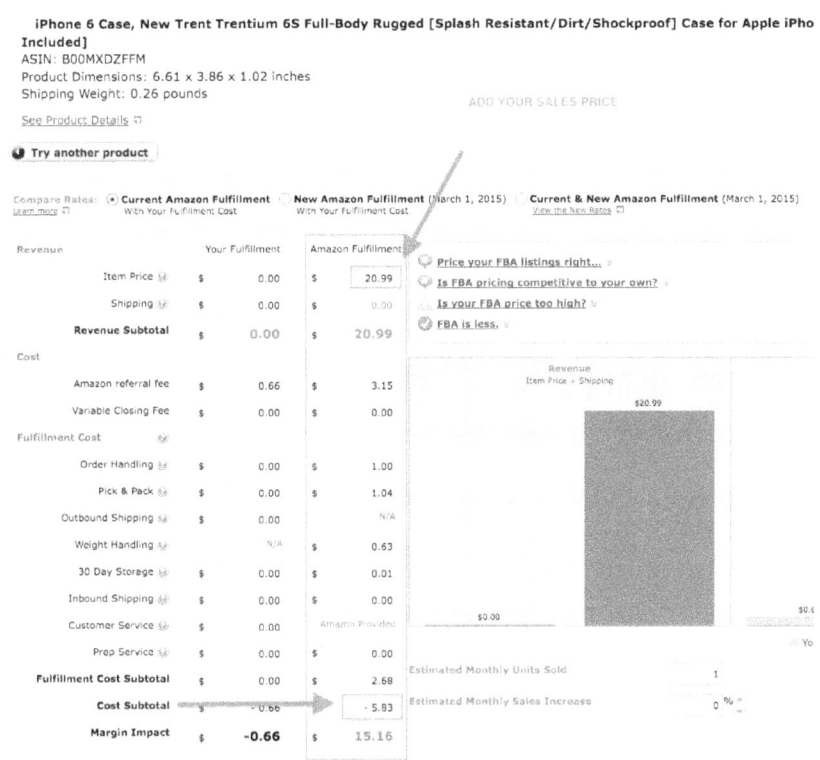

Amazon's total fee is $5.83 if you want to sell this product at $20.99. This means that Amazon will pay you $15.16 when they have sold and shipped 1 unit. Ofcourse you still need to deduct the unit cost, shipping charges per unit and your cost per sale (advertisement).

Chapter Two – How to Set Up Your Seller Central Account

In this chapter, we are going to go through the nuts and bolts of setting up your Seller's account on Amazon. There are two approaches we'll take a look at: creating a Seller Central account if you live **in the U.S.** and setting up an account if you live **outsidethe U.S.** I will also walk through how to set up payment options if you do not have a U.S. bank account and need to consider alternative options.

Creating Your Seller Central Account

To begin, head over to **Amazon Seller Central** at http://sellercentral.amazon.com. This address takes you to the Seller Central homepage. You'll see a log-in area, as well as a number of "Learn More" boxes that you can explore to really get familiar with the interface. Feel free to explore these at your leisure. Click on "Register now" to setup your account.

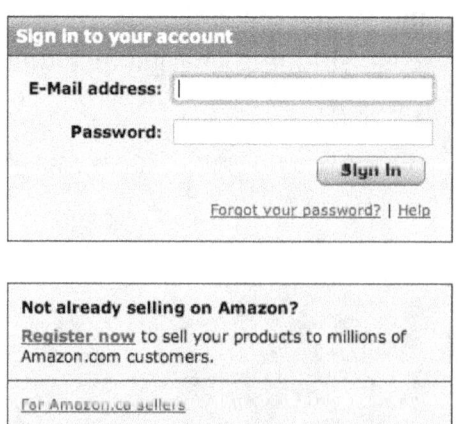

To set up your account, you will need:

An Email Address – The email address you use to set up your Seller Central account is going to be the one Amazon uses to communicate with you about transactions. You are also going to receive notifications and communications from your customers through this email. As such, you may want to use an email address that is dedicated solely to your new business, rather than a personal one you already use for communications with friends, social networks, etc.

> *Pro Tip— Keep your account separate from other accounts you may have on Amazon. For example, you may have a personal account that you use to buy products for yourself or you may have one that you use to access Instant Video and other media. It's a good idea to keep things separate to avoid confusion on your end and make sure that you put forward as professional an image as possible.*

A Bank Account – A bank account is required so that you can receive payments for all your transactions. U.S. residents with U.S. bank accounts can use their existing accounts for this. If you live outside the U.S., you'll need to explore some helpful alternatives to receive payments. We'll walk through those later on in this chapter.

An Address – You are also going to need an address to set up your account. This address will be used for receiving shipments and customer returns.

A Seller Name – You also need to select a Seller Name for your account. This will serve as an important branding component in your new business. We'll walk through some of the ins and outs of choosing a great seller name further on in this chapter.

A Phone Number – Even with the ease of email and online

communications, sometimes it's just better to pick up a phone and talk with another human being. Have a phone number that you can use to communicate with Amazon as needed.

A Credit Card – Setting up a Professional account requires a credit card. As of this writing, the monthly charge for a Professional account is $39.99, which is currently deferred for the first month during a Free Trial period. Once you get your business going, chances are that your sales will cover this monthly charge, but plan on having a $39.99 charge go through on this card each month once you pass your Free Trial period.

A Business Entity – It is a good idea to set up a business entity to handle your Amazon products. Your best option is to set up an LLC, or Limited Liability Corporation. You can register a new business as an LLC almost anywhere in the U.S.

You can also start selling products as an individual. Once you have recurring sales you can setup a business entity.

The Step-by-Step Setup Process

Once you have everything ready that you need to set up your account, you can start plugging in your information into Seller Central. First off, you'll need to register as a user on the site.

Step One – Click on the "Register Now" button located below the log-in interface. This takes you to the registry page where you'll see a "Sell as a Professional" option and a "Sell as an Individual" option. My recommendation is that you go with "Sell as a Professional". As mentioned earlier, the "Sell as a Professional" option does involve a monthly charge, but you will get all the leeway you need to really take advantage of what you are going to learn in this course. "Sell as an Individual" limits you to 40 sales a month and limits what you can do.

Step Two – Enter your registration information. Click on "Sell as a Professional". This takes you to a data entry page where you will enter:

- Your Name

- Your Business Email Address

- Your Business Legal Name

You will also be asked to select a password for the account. Select one that is complex enough to evade those dreaded hackers and make note of it in a safe place. You will also need to check the box that indicates that you agree with the Amazon Services Business Solutions agreement. Click this box, and click on the highlighted Amazon Services Business Solutions agreement title if you want to review the agreement in detail.

Step Three – Click on 'Continue'. This will take you to a Welcome screen where you will next enter your Seller Information.

Step Four – Enter your Seller Information. On the next page, start plugging in all the Seller information you have at the ready for your new business. Your Display Name is particularly important. Choose one that fits your niche. It should not be your brand name. Instead, use a general ID that can include your name. After you have entered all the information, click on "Save & Continue".

Step Five – Enter your payment information. You can use a credit card, a debit card, or even a pre-paid card. Just remember that, at least at first, you may incur a monthly charge on the card.

Step Six – Verify your identity. If you've ever changed an email password or tried to access an important account through a new device, you've been through this process. Essentially, Amazon just wants to make sure that you are who you say you are and are not setting up bulk accounts.

Step Seven – Enter your business information. This part of the process is where you enter the information Amazon needs to pay you and cover their tax liability to your business. Click on "Launch Interview Wizard" and answer all the questions. You can use your personal information if you do not have an LLC set up.

Step Eight – Click 'Continue'. And that's it! You've set up your Seller Central account.

As we proceed through this program, you'll learn *a lot* more about the Seller Central account and how you can take advantage of it. We will cover all of this in greater detail further on.

How to Create a Seller Central Account Outside the U.S.

Amazon supports businesses located in the following countries:

- USA
- UK
- Austria
- Belgium
- Cyprus
- Estonia
- Finland
- France
- Germany
- Greece
- Ireland
- Italy
- Luxembourg
- Malta
- Portugal
- Slovakia
- Slovenia
- Spain
- Canada
- Australia

- New Zealand
- Hong Kong
- India

If you live in any of these countries, you are good to go with the step-by-step setup we went through in the previous section. If not, you will need to take a slightly different approach, but one that is not too difficult.

Getting a U.S. Bank Account

As a first step, check with your local bank and see if they can set you up with a U.S.-based account. It is important to make sure that this is not just what is known as a "U.S. Funds" account. If your local bank cannot do this, check to see if there are any major international banks in your town or city that can accommodate this request.

In some cases, you won't be able to set up a U.S.-based bank account. If not, there are a number of third party providers you can turn to that can act as a facilitator or go-between for you with a U.S. bank.

Alternatives to U.S. Bank Accounts

By and large, the best option for you if you live outside the U.S. and do not have a U.S. account is to go through an organization called Payoneer. Payoneer provides you with a debit card linked to a U.S.-based bank account, thereby qualifying you as a Seller on Amazon.

Setting Up an Account on Payoneer

Setting up an account on Payoneer is straightforward. Let's walk through it step by step. First off, go to Payoneer.com and click on the "Sign Up for an Account" button you'll see on the homepage.

Step One – Enter your basic information. In the first data entry page, enter your full name, your email address and your date of birth. Click on 'next' once this is done.

Step Two –Enter your contact information. On the next page, select your country of residence from the drop-down menu provided. Then enter your address and a phone number where you can be reached. Click on 'next'.

Step Three – Choose a password and security question. On the next page, you need to select a password and a security question and answer that will be used to verify your account. As always, make sure that your password involves a number of characters and make sure to include at least one numeral. Click on 'next'.

Step Four – Enter an I.D. Payoneer needs to verify your identity through an official government identification. Enter all pertinent information, and also enter a shipping address if it is different from the personal address you used earlier. You also need to click on the box that states you agree with Payoneer's policies. Click on 'Finish'.

With that quick setup, you should be all set. If you have any difficulties, reach out to Payoneer customer service for additional help on getting an account going with them.

Chapter Three – How To Pick Money-Making Products on Amazon

So, you've set up your Seller Central account. Now what are you going to sell? There is an *endless* world of products out there, and parsing through that may seem a bit overwhelming at first. The good news is I can walk your through some key tips that will help you isolate the best categories and select the best products to drive your new Amazon FBA business.

Restricted Products vs. Non-Restricted Products

There is an important distinction for you to realize right off the bat with Amazon— they categorize some products as "restricted" while others are not restricted. Now, selling restricted products can be quite lucrative in the long run, but with your first go-round as you're learning your way through FBA, it's best to stick with non-restricted items.

Restricted Products on Amazon

Restricted products on Amazon are items that require additional approval for you to sell them. These products may be specialty items, complex products, or may involve a more complex selling

model (as with textbook rentals, for example) and Amazon just wants to ensure that you are the right seller for that category.

Their criteria for approval varies from product category to product category. As you evolve in your Amazon FBA know-how, you may want to start exploring these categories and the requirements they involve by visiting Amazon's help page on the topic. For the time being so you know what to avoid, here's a list of restricted Amazon product categories:

- Automotive & Powersports
- Beauty
- Clothing & Accessories
- Collectible Books
- Entertainment Collectibles
- Fine Art
- Gift Cards
- Grocery & Gourmet Foods
- Health & Personal Care
- Industrial & Scientific
- Jewelry
- Luggage & Travel Accessories
- Major Appliances
- Sexual Wellness
- Shoes, Handbags & Sunglasses
- Sports Collectibles
- Textbook Rentals
- Toys & Games (holiday approval products only)
- Watches
- Wine

So What Do You Sell?

In short, *physical products. Real products.* You want to sell actual physical products people want and need. That may sound pat or glib, but it's a perfect summary of what I want you to go after here.

Now, some people encourage an approach known as long tail selling, which is essentially compiling a vast array of incredibly niche products. Even if you sell only one or two products in each category, you still end up with high sales in the gestalt... or so the theory goes. In actuality, this approach ends up being a logistical nightmare, cost prohibitive to start up, and not the right option for a firsttimer.

Instead, here's my suggestion— go with what you know. Take a look around you, at your life and your hobbies. Take an inventory of what you use in your home or in your office. What are the items you really resonate with, the products you really understand?

Why this approach? Because it puts you in a better position to sell the product and deliver the most effective customer service. Selling what you actually like gives you:

Differentiators in a crowded marketplace— In short, you will know what makes this item special. You already have firsthand experience with what differentiates this product from others in its space.

A unique perspective on marketing— As a user and consumer of this product yourself, you are personally engaged in it and thus much more likely to know what other consumers want to see when it comes to this product.

A built-in network— Let's say you're an equestrian. You probably know a number of other riders, too, right? These friends, this *network*, is a great resource as you build your business. Your friends can write reviews, test products, and give you feedback. It's like your own R&D department.

So as you look around and consider what products will work best for you and your Amazon FBA business, ask yourself the following:

- What have I bought for the house or the office in the last month or so?

- What do I love to do? Is there anything from my hobbies that could be the right one?

As you ask yourself these questions, jot down some initial ideas. Go through this list of ideas and see if you can shake out four or five general product categories, be they tech, cooking, etc. These categories will be key later on as I walk you through final product selection and figuring out what your first best seller will be.

What is Private Labeling?

Before I get into further detail on product selection, let's take a moment here to discuss exactly what private labeling is. I've told you the basics about Amazon FBA and Seller Central,but it will help if you really understand why I am asking you to take this approach.

Private Labeling is this— creating a BRAND from a previously manufactured product. You're not inventing the light bulb here, you're not creating something from scratch. Private labeling involves finding a viable, ready-to-go product and giving it your own unique spin.

Why this approach? Private labeling gives you an array of advantages, including:

- Pricing control
- Marketing control
- Brand control

That's a lot of control. This approach places the reins in your hands and allows you to go as far as you want with your new business. Sound appealing?

Now for the legwork. You have a definition for private labeling on hand, but how do you get it done? Private labeling involves three basic components:

Identifying an ideal opportunity— As discussed, you are already keeping your eyes open for the things around you that may work. I'll get into zeroing in on the best opportunities in some of the following sections.

Sourcing a supplier— You need a consistent and reliable supplier of your product. I'll walk you through this in Chapter Four.

Branding and marketing – Once you have a supply of your ideal product ready to go, you will need to label it, package it, and market it effectively. All of these choices define your brand and define how effective you'll be in your space. No worries, I'll take you through this as well.

Common Questions About Private Labeling

As I teach and share my ideas about Amazon FBA and private labeling, I hear many of the same questions time and time again. One that often comes up is *why don't the suppliers do this themselves?* Well, they are by and large wholesalers. Their whole approach is to sell at cost to individuals (like you) who will then sell an item at retail.

Other questions that come up often have to do with logistics—specifically, *how much and how much of a bother?* To answer the first part, not much. You can get your private labeling business up and running with a small first investment of around $1200. Of course to do this you'll need some savvy negotiating techniques. Second, remember, you will be working with Amazon's Fulfillment program.

You won't need to store stock in your home, ship things yourself, etc. My approach is about as hassle-free as this gets.

So, are you ready now to find your opportunity? Let's take a look at how to identify a bestseller.

Researching theTop 100 Best Sellers on Amazon

Your first step in zeroing in on your best seller is researching the Best Sellers already on Amazon. Amazon maintains easily accessible Top 100 lists in all of their product categories. Visit the Amazon Best Seller page and look for one of the product categories you selected for yourself as a potential product category for your business in the previous section.

Start looking through the list— do you see any items that appeal to you, maybe ones you already hit on as a potential product for yourself? Go through the Top 100 for your product category and start to get a sense of what this niche is like.

What is appealing to people?

What are their primary interests and concerns?

This will give you a general overview of your niche and serves as the starting point for zeroing in on a product and identifying a best seller.

How to Identify Potential Products from Amazon's Best Sellers List

As you look through the list of Best Sellers in your category, ask yourself: What defines a Best Seller? What are the characteristics that set it apart from others, potentially making it a viable best seller for your private labeling business?

Every Best Seller has a particular set of qualities that sets it apart:

- **Best-selling ranking(BSR)**

→BSR from 0 to 500   = VERY GOOD

Product Details
  Shipping Weight: 4.2 ounces (View shipping rates and policies)
  ASIN:
  Item model number: NT636CR-S
  Average Customer Review: ☆☆☆☆☆ ✔ (2,388 customer reviews)
  Amazon Best Sellers Rank: #96 in Cell Phones & Accessories (See Top 100 in Cell Phones & Accessories)
        #9 in Cell Phones & Accessories > Cases > Cases
        #82 in Cell Phones & Accessories > Accessories

→BSR from 501 to 2000 = GOOD

Product Details
  Color: Black
  Product Dimensions: 2 x 1.5 x 2.5 inches
  Shipping Weight: 2.4 ounces (View shipping rates and policies)
  Shipping: Currently, item can be shipped only within the U.S.
  ASIN:
  Item model number: Aero Black
  Average Customer Review: ☆☆☆☆☆ (219 customer reviews)
  Amazon Best Sellers Rank: #1,111 in Cell Phones & Accessories (See Top 100 in Cell Phones & Accessories)
        #32 in Cell Phones & Accessories > Accessories > Car Accessories > Car Cradles & Mounts > Car Mounts
        #48 in Cell Phones & Accessories > Accessories > Cradles, Mounts & Stands

→ I prefer to go with products with BSR's between 500 and 2000

A high rank but with few reviews

- Look for products with less than 400 customer reviews!

- When you have found a 'potential product' on the best-seller list, type the primary keyword on Amazon and check the first 16 listings on page one. If you can find 3 listings with BSR less than 2000, then it's a potential product that I will add to my list.

- An ideal selling price

- Branding potential for private labeling

- A healthy profit margin (50-55%)

Each of these qualities will make more sense as I take you deeper and deeper into the Amazon FBA process and product selection, but I'll walk you through a few basics on each of these right now.

Ranking

It seems pretty self-explanatory that a product with a best-selling ranking is a potential opportunity. Where things get interesting is when we look at the ranking of *related items.* Take a pair of Beats headphones. Is this item selling well because it's driven by a popular brand, namely Dr. Dre, or is it the headphones themselves that are selling well? You want to look at related products and determine whether generic items in a niche are selling like hotcakes or whether or not it's just the marquee name of an item that is driving sales.

Reviews

This may seem a bit counterintuitive— you want to find and isolate products and their related products with *fewer reviews (less than 400).* Why? This is where opportunity lies. It means that an item is selling but that a dialogue hasn't developed around that item. It's not in the zeitgeist yet, so to speak. This is where YOU can step in and drive a conversation. And more importantly, create a brand.

Selling Price

What is the ideal price for a private labeling business? You want to keep an eye out for products somewhere between $15 and $50. Anything less than $15 isn't worth it, (unless you have an exclusive product). More than $50 alienates a lot of consumers.

Branding Potential

Will you be able to make this product your own in some way? Is branding it actually a real prospect? You could never, for example, rebrand an iPad. That has Apple's branding all over it and always will. Look for products that give you some room to grow in this respect.

A Healthy Profit Margin

I will take you through some more specifics down the line that will make this aspect clearer, but for now start thinking about products that have the potential to deliver a profit margin of at least 40 to 55%.

DeterminingPrimary and Secondary Keywords for Your Product

Another aspect that you need to consider as you zero in on a product are its primary and secondary keywords. How effective these keywords are will determine how easily someone can pull up your product on Amazon.

Let's run you through an example. Take a cordless phone charger, one of those small-handheld phone accessories that deliver much-needed power to your cell when you are out and about and nowhere near an outlet or your regular charger. Say you are a consumer looking for this particular item. You don't *quite* know what to call it, right? "Cordless phone charger" sounds kind of right, but then "portable phone charger" could work, too. Which one is your consumer going to plug into

Google to find that product?

In order for your product to have the highest profile, you need to make sure that you have the best primary and secondary keywords for that product nailed down. To do this, you can use one of the most effective tools in the world of online marketing— Google Adwords.

As you may know, Google Adwords is an interface created by Google that helps online businesses manage and track online advertising and marketing. One of the central tools in this interface is the Google Adwords Keyword Planner. Click on the link and head over to the Keyword Planner.

If you do not have an AdWords account, you'll need to set one up. You can see a 'Create an account' link at the top right-hand corner of the page. All you need to do is plug in some basic information like your email address and your time zone. Once this is done, go ahead and sign in to AdWords.

On the Keyword Planner home page, you'll see a list of options on the left-hand side of the page. Click on "Search for new keyword and ad group ideas." On the next page, you'll see several input data fields. Enter the name of your product in the "Your Product and service" field. For this example, let's use our cordless phone charger. Click on "Get ideas" at the bottom.

Plugging in our car mount holder as our product pulls up a list of keyword groups or "ad groups" by relevance. If you click on each of these highlighted group names, you will see the list of all the keywords within that group, listed by relevance.

Ad group ideas   Keyword ideas

Search terms		Avg. monthly searches	Competition
car phone holder		2,900	High
car mount holder		110	High

Keyword (by relevance)		Avg. monthly searches	Competition
phone holder for car		2,900	High
cell phone holder for car		2,400	High
cell phone car holder		590	High
car cell phone holder		390	High
phone car holder		390	High

These keywords popped up. You can see that our heaviest hitter is "car phone holder". Working with the first suggestion and the third — "phone holder for car"— are the best approach.

Now let's head over to Amazon. On the Amazon home page, entering the first keyword term in the search interface pulls up a list of products. Open the first several products in their own tabs, then look at each of them in turn and check out their Best Seller ranking, which is located under the Product Details section of the product page.

How do those numbers look? If your result is something along the lines of BSR #500 to 2000, you've found a potential opportunity that is selling well. If those numbers are less stellar (and they can be way less stellar) you may need to start looking into other potential opportunities.

Checking the Best Seller Rank History

There's a great tool out there that I use all the time to check the Best Seller Rank or BSR history for an item. That tool is a website called **CamelCamelCamel.com**.

CamelCamelCamel, or "Three Camel", offers a range of tools for interacting with the Amazon space. I find one offering of theirs in particular to be the most beneficial when working with Amazon— their Browser Add-on. As of this writing, they only have add-ons for Google Chrome, Firefox, and Safari, so you will need to be using one of those browsers on your computer to take advantage of this tool.

What this add-on does is pretty amazing. Once you install the add-on, you'll see a small "camel" icon in your browser bar. When you visit an Amazon product listing, clicking on this camel pulls up the entire price history chart for that product.

It's an unbelievably valuable tool for your purposes here. With one click, you get an entire overview of that product's performance. How valuable do you think that will be as you begin to assess products and see which one will be the best product to launch your brand on Amazon FBA?

I especially like Three Camel's browser add-on because it gives me away to spot any false spikes in a product's sales. Let's say you find a product that ranks high on Amazon and that you think has some legs as a potential product. What if those high sales are not consistent or historical? What if they are just the result of a one-time promotion or the initial launch of the product? By looking at the *entire* sales history of the product, you can get a much more realistic idea of whether a product has legs or not.

So give 3C (=CamelCamelCamel) a try. I guarantee it will help you as you continue to explore Amazon FBA and build your brand.

Chapter Four - How To Find High Quality Suppliers

Your next step in the process now that you've zeroed in on a product that has the potential to go far on Amazon is to find yourself a high-quality supplier. There are a number of ways in which you can do this and I will walk you through each of these in turn.

Finding Suppliers with Google

You look for a lot of what you need using Google already, yes? Why not also use it to find your supplier? There is a rub to this, however, and that is that, as we discussed earlier, the suppliers you need are not necessarily the best self-promoters or marketers. As mentioned, their business model is built around the wholesale world, which is pretty insular. They are not going to promote their business as widely as you might like, and they may well not be in the first few pages of a Google search.

As a consumer yourself, you likely don't go much further than the first few pages of Google search results before settling on something. For your purposes here, you are going to have to go further and dig a little deeper to find the right supplier.

The good news is that using Google can be really useful for you in your search. The vast majority of quality suppliers out there are within reach via Google; you just need to use some tricks of the trade to find them.

Tricks for Streamlining Your Supplier Search on Google

There are a number of ways in which you can run a Google search for a supplier in the most efficient way possible. These include:

- Using quotation marks
- Excluding some search criteria, and
- Utilizing the right phrasing

Let's start off with the last option, using the right phrasing. You may be aware of the fact that using as little extraneous language as possible is the best way to run a Google search. For example, if I were looking for a new pair of sneakers from Nike, I wouldn't run a search for "new pair of sneakers from Nike." I would just search for "Nike sneakers" or even "Nike men's sneakers." Any extraneous words will just pull up a lot of useless sites that are only peripherally related to what I am looking for. Make sure that you use quotation marks around this keyword phrase to maintain its specificity. This tells Google that you are looking for **exactly** that phrase and nothing somewhat related. So...

Tip #1 – As you run your Google search, use very specific phrasing that defines what you need exactly. Use quotation marks!

Secondly, you want to include some words or phrases that are going to take you to the people you need, namely suppliers. To do this, include the following in your search:

- Private label
- Supplier
- Manufacturer
- Wholesale

Including one of these along with your exact keyword phrase

in quotation marks will get you to the search results you need that much sooner.

Tip #2 – Include the industry phrases that relate to suppliers, namely supplier, wholesale, and private label.

Finally, use the exclusion formula to exclude any sites that won't benefit you. A lot of wholesale businesses may have information posted on discount sales sites or even on Facebook. Excluding sites like these just makes things go more quickly.

The exclusion formula for blocking results from a website during a Google search is **–site:[site name]**. For example, if I didn't want Nextag.com included in my search results, I would include **–site:nextag.com** in my search criteria. In general, I think it's a good idea to exclude the following sites:

- Amazon.com
- Bizrate.com
- Thefind.com
- Blogspot.com
- Nextag.com
- Facebook.com
- Shopzilla.com
- Overstock.com

Tip #3 – Exclude sales sites and social networks from search results using –site:[site name]

Finding US suppliers on ThomasNet.com

Another highly valuable tool you can use during your search for a quality supplier is the website ThomasNet.com. This site is a "supplier discovery resource" or, in other words, a giant database of suppliers that you can scour through. ThomasNet.com offers six ways to approach a search, but for your purposes you will only need one: their Supplier Discovery platform.

Using the Supplier Discovery Platform on ThomasNet.com

When you click on the Supplier Discovery tab at the top of the ThomasNet.com home page, you will be taken to a search page with data entry fields. The first criteria they ask you is what you want to find your product by. In other words, it lets you choose between searching by product/service category, a brand name, a company name, or something called a UNSPSC Commodity, which is basically a code that defines a specific manufactured product. This organization— the United Nations Standard Products and Services Code— classifies all the products out there into categories and codes. Windshield wipers, for example, are classified under the code '251715'.

For your intents and purposes, however, you just want to search by Product/Service Category. It's best to start out with a very basic term. If I wanted to find a book stand manufacturer, I might just plug in the term "stand." ThomasNet.com actually pulls up a drop-down list of suggestions, including everything from cake stands to camera stands. Select the one that matches your needs. You can also narrow your search criteria by selecting items in the Optional Section #3, which include geographical specifications and certifications. These are not really applicable here, so I would just bypass the Optional section and click on "View Suppliers".

This will take you to a detailed list of all suppliers on ThomasNet who produce that product. The great thing about these search results is that you get a summary of each supplier on the list, so you can skim through their qualifications right away. As you go through the list, you can also click on the highlighted name of any company that looks appealing to visit their individual page, where you can glean even more information about them. You can also run a comparison between any of the companies by checking the select box next to their name and then clicking on the "Compare" button at the top of the list.

Finding Overseas Suppliers on Alibaba.com

Some of you may have heard about Alibaba.com in the news recently. It's one of the biggest companies in China and a significant portion of it was purchased by Yahoo a few years back, so it's regularly highlighted in tech news articles.

For your intents and purposes, it's another great resource that you can use specifically to find suppliers outside of the U.S. This enormous database serves as a hub for manufacturers around the world and retailers to meet up and do business. If you have any questions about doing business with overseas manufacturers, I recommend visiting Alibaba.com's Safety and Security Center. This Help Center subcategory has a lot of information on maintaining a safe account on Alibaba.com and finding the most reliable suppliers.

Utilizing Alibaba.com Effectively

As a starting point, go to Alibaba.com and create an account for your business. This is a must as you will not be allowed to contact any suppliers without an account. Once you have your account in place, you can start exploring all of their resources.

There are a number of approaches you can take to search for a supplier on Alibaba.com. I believe the best way is to use their **Advanced Search** interface. Select the Products tab, and make sure you select the toggle for "exact match" beneath the search input field. Then enter your keyword phrase for your product in the search input field and click on the Search button. You can also narrow your search by country, but I prefer to get the widest ranging list of suppliers to start out with.

On the search results page, you can start narrowing down your results. The site offers a series of Sort By options:

- Gold Supplier

- Onsite Check

- Assessed Supplier

- Trade Assurance

The first three of these are critical. Select them to narrow the search results down to the suppliers who meet these qualifications. Those first three criteria help ensure that you find a quality supplier. You may have an interest in selecting the Trade Assurance option, which provides some assurances that you get your product and that you can potentially get a partial refund if need be, but I personally do not use this to find a supplier.

So, now you have a refined list with more qualified suppliers. On each supplier's listing you'll see various icons indication that they are either a Gold Supplier, engage in Onsite Checks, or are an Assessed Supplier. What each of these means in detail is:

Gold Supplier – an accreditation given to only the most serious and dedicated suppliers on Alibaba. These companies have been vetted by a third-party security provider. You can also see how many years a company has maintained these credentials for. I recommend working with suppliers who have a gold supplier batch of +3 years

Ningbo Jiangbei MG Electronics Co.,... ⌄

China (Mainland)　　Contact Details ▸

US $28,000 Trade Assurance Amount

67.1% Response Rate

Contact Supplier　　🕐 Chat Now!

Onsite Check – Onsite check covers suppliers located in mainland China. It basically serves as an assurance to those who may have concerns about doing business with Chinese manufacturers. All of these companies are Gold Suppliers and have had their business licenses verified by a third party. Alibaba.com employees have also conducted site visits to these companies to ensure that everything is above board.

Supplier Assessment – Companies who have had supplier assessments done on them have been visited by third-party inspectors who have looked closely at their sites and practices and drafted a detailed report.

You can also see on the left hand side of the page several organizations listed under "Certification". These organizations include the FDA or Federal Department of Agriculture in the U.S. and the CE/EU, the European Union body that oversees product safety. Depending on your product, you may want to narrow your search further by selecting some of these options. For example, you would not want to sell, say, cookware in the States that does not have FDA approval.

You will also see an input box at the top of the search results labeled "Minimum Order". Narrowing a search by the minimum order amount defined by a supplier isn't that helpful since by and large these minimums are negotiable. You don't even need to select the toggle right next to that box, labeled "Online". This narrows down your list to the suppliers who are online right at that moment, so that you can potentially chat with them. Since you may well be dealing with suppliers in a different time zone, this is seldom useful.

Assessing Suppliers on Alibaba.com

Now that you've narrowed down your list to the best of the best, you can start looking at individual suppliers in greater detail. A few things I want you to keep in mind as you do this:

Review Contact Information – Check out the supplier's contact information and see if they have a website. Visiting any business' website can give you a very clear idea of what they're about and can tell you whether or not you are dealing with professionals.

Read through the Product Details – As you scroll through the list of products and their suppliers, click on the highlighted title of any product that looks appealing. This takes you to the product detail page where you can review the product more closely, get a closer look at the company, and even see some of their other products.

Select Favorites – As you go through the search results, click on the Favorites icon just below the product picture if that listing appeals to you. This will help you keep track of which were appealing and which were no-gos.

Run a Comparison – After you have compiled at least 15-20 Favorites, run a comparison between all of them. Click on the My Alibaba tab at the top of the page and select My Favorites.

As you hover your mouse over each product image, you'll see some selection options pop up. Select "Add to Compare". Each product will load into a Compare window on the right hand of the screen. Click on Compare when you're done and you can assess their qualifications side by side, including accepted payment methods and more.

After you have done all this, you should be able to winnow your list down to an elite few. At this point you will want to reach out to these suppliers to make initial contact and begin the negotiation process. The good news is that you can message all of your preferred sellers at once from My Favorites:

- Go to My Favorites and click on the Products tab

- Click on Select All if you want to message all of the suppliers on your My Favorites list or select the companies you prefer by checking their boxes

- Then click on Contact Supplier

This will open up an email directed to all of the selected suppliers. Alibaba.com will fill in your subject field with an automatic message when you message an individual supplier, but you will need to plug in a generic subject line here. Enter a Subject line that can apply to all of the suppliers such as "general inquiry" and then draft your message. Keep it as professional as possible.

You can also message each supplier individually. This is sometimes the better approach because you can use specifics about their product, pricing, and minimum order requirements to begin your negotiations. If you click on Contact Supplier on an individual listing, Alibaba.com will automatically fill in the Subject field with a generic inquiry specific to that product. In the message field, draft your email around the specifics you need to see a deal happen.

For example, if the supplier's minimum order is 2500 but you aren't ready to commit to that many, you can mention in this message that you are committed to moving ahead, but want to start with a lower number for the first round. Don't lowball them, and keep it reasonable. A supplier who has a 2500 minimum order requirement is not going to want to produce 10 for you.

Also make sure you're familiar with the supplier's pricing range for that product. This, of course, might change depending on the volume of your order, but you want to make sure you have a good idea of their range so you don't accidentally stick yourself with an inflated price.

Finally, you will want to request some samples once you've whittled your list of suppliers down to a select few. Ask 3 to 5 suppliers to send you a sample. The sample itself is, of course, typically free of charge, but you will need to cover the shipping. A shipment from China should go on DHL or UPS and should take about 3 to 4 days to reach the U.S. You should budget for about $35-50 in shipping costs for each of these samples. As of now, there are no custom fees and taxes on samples under around $70. Take your time to look them over carefully and determine which supplier is going to get you the best product for your money.

Chapter Five – How to Create Your Brand

At this point, I hope that you have one product that you believe in and that you think can go the mile with you in Amazon FBA. Focusing on that one product, I want to talk to you now about what is probably one of the most crucial aspects of this entire process— branding.

Even if you've never worked in marketing or advertising, you know what a brand is. In fact, as a member of this modern world, you're probably more keenly attuned to brand than you realize. Brands are everywhere, and not just on products. Pop stars are brands, even politicians. If you look around, you probably know a lot more about this than you think and are perfectly positioned to drive your own brand.

Selecting the Right Brand Name

As a starting point, you have to choose an effective brand name. Now, don't trip yourself up on this one. Many people who are starting a private labeling business get stuck on this point, but you don't want to overthink this one. Sure, it helps to have a great name, but it's not "make or break" territory. Choose one that:

Suits your niche - there's language in your niche and you want to pick a name that fits that language. Think of all the i-this and e-that products in the tech world. Take a look at the brand names around you and select something that works with them.

Has an available domain –Visit www.godaddy.com and see if your brand name's domain name has already been claimed.

While you won't be using your domain name right away, you do want the option to leverage it somewhere down the line.

You will also want to research your brand name on Amazon; after all, you would want another seller with the same brand, right? Just go to the Amazon home page and plug in your brand name to the search bar. If it comes up, rethink your brand name.

Run a trademark search as well for your brand name. A brand name that already exists as the registered trademark of another company is not going to do your new business any favors. The U.S. Patent and Trademark Office maintains a great search interface online known as the **Trademark Electronic Search System** or **TESS**. Through TESS, you can run a Basic Word Mark Search for a brand name and see if this name has been trademarked by another company.

Picking a Name For Your Product

You are also going to need to select a viable product name for your product. You will use this mainly on your product label and packaging, but not necessarily even on your Amazon listing. When selecting your product name, keep a few things in consideration:

Keep it simple and clear – You want your customers to know what your product is after all.

Make sure it suits your niche – Again, you want something that is in keeping with your niche, just as with your brand name.

Use your primary keyword – If possible, incorporate your primary keyword. This will give you an added oomph with Amazon customer searches and will encourage consumers to click on your product.

Outsourcing Your Brand Design Work

Chances are you will need a graphic designer on your team. Unless you are a trained designer or else the supplier you eventually decide to work with offers design services, you are going to need a graphics specialist who can help with the visual components of your brand. What are the visual components of your brand? I'll take you through the basic design specifications you will need to forward to your designer.

Branding Design Specs

Your designer is going to be creating the product and packaging labels for your product. To do this, he or she will need:

- Exact dimensions of the product and packaging

- The text to be included on labels and packaging

You also want to let your designer know which file type works best for your needs. A wide range of image file types can work, including JPGs, PNGs, and PSDs, but you should choose one that you are familiar with and can work easily with.

Sourcing Your Designer

There are some great freelancer websites out there that you can use to find a reasonably priced graphic designer. Two of the best options are oDesk and elance. These sites allow you to post job ads that candidates then respond to. You can interview designers, review portfolios, and even pay them through these helpful sites.

First off, you'll need to set up an account on either oDesk.com or Elance.com, and then fill out a job posting. You can leave it open and wait and see if some viable designers come forward, but the more proactive option is to search through the database of freelancers and invite specific designers to interview for your job. Make sure that you look through their histories, ratings, and profiles so that you can glean the most information about them before starting the interview process. Using Skype for a video interview is a great way to go, as "putting a face to the name" can give you better insight into who you'll be working with.

You can also use 99designs.com, which will be a moreexpensive option. However, you'll find great graphic designers on 99designs.com

Chapter Six— How To Create A High Converting and Optimized Amazon Product Listing

At this point, I want to go back into Amazon Seller Central and talk about setting up your Amazon product listing, or product page. This is the page where consumers will come to review your product and make a purchasing decision. There are certain things that you need to pay attention to that can make this page as appealing to your consumer as possible. If you optimize everything you have control of via your Amazon Seller Central account, you are going to convert a lot more visitors to your page into purchasers.

The Four Key Components of the Amazon Product Listing

Each Amazon product listing, or "product detail page", has four key components that let visitors know everything they need to know about a product. These four components are:

- The Product's title

- Its description

- Associated Images, and

- "Other" fields (these vary depending on the product)

Creating a New Product Listing on Amazon

Setting up a new product listing on Amazon for your product involves several steps. I'll walk you through them right now.

- Step One –Click on the Inventory menu and select "Add product" from the drop-down menu

- Step Two -Click on "Create a new product"

amazon seller central   INVENTORY   ORDERS   ADVERTISING   REPORTS   PERFORMANCE

Add a Product

The product you are adding may already exist on Amazon. Search our catalog for the product you want to sell and save yourself some time.
Learn more | Video Tutorials | Upload multiple products

Find it on Amazon

Results are limited to the first 1,000 pages.

  Enter your product name, UPC, EAN, ISBN or ASIN | Search

If it is not in Amazon's catalog: Create a new product

- **Step Three – Choose a category for your product**

  Now I want to take a moment here to talk about catego-ries on Amazon in more detail. Products can fit into a lot of different categories on Amazon and choosing one can be somewhat confusing.

  Ideally, you want to place your product in a sub-category of the top-level category where you first found the similar product that inspired your product selection. If it is a wok, for example, you likely saw the original wok that inspired your choice in the "Home" category.

  Click on the top-level category that applies to your product and explore the sub-categories. Chances are there will not be a sub-category that defines your prod-uct exactly, but choose one that fits as closely as possi-ble. Check your competitors' categories/subcategories as well.

- **Step Four - Enter your product information**

  After you choose the right category for your product, Amazon takes you to their "Listing Assistant". This in-terface involves several tabs of information fields that you need to fill in about your product. The tabs listed all depend on what product category you selected. Just concern yourself with the ones labeled with a red asterisk indicating that they are required fields.

Required Tabs

I want to walk you through each of the tabs that contain required info so that you can get your Product page in top shape.

The Vital Info Tab

One of these tabs with required fields is the Vital Info tab. In the Vital Info tab, you need to input:

Your Product Name (aka Your Product Title)

- Primary and secondary keywords along with some Benefit/Feature sales copy

- The Product Manufacturer (your brand name)

- A UPC or EAN (a barcode with a 12-digit number that identifies your product). There are many UPC suppliers. Check Ebay.com, SpeedyBarcodes.com, ...

Regarding the UPC, you can easily get one of these for your product online. They are issued by a not-for-profit organization in the U.S., the GS1. As your business grows, you can add product variations to one GS 1 identification code, as well, if you start exploring size or color variations of a product.

A few notesnow on the necessity of adding some Benefit/Feature sales copy to the tail of your primary and secondary keywords. Think of the copy you enter here as a taster of what's to come on the rest of your page. You need this, and you want it to be compelling so that page visitors keep reading. I'll walk you through some copywriting tips in greater detail later on, but here's an example of what I'm talking about for now:

Makeup Removerfrom L'Oreal – Organic, Waterproof and Refreshing! 4 oz.

The Offer Tab

More required fields come up under the Offer tab. Here you need to enter:

- The condition of your item (new, of course!)

- The price (Don't overthink this— you can always adjust it later on)

- The quantity (Since your inventory is logged through Amazon FBA you don't need to worry about this. Just plug in "125" to fill in the spot.)

- Your Shipping Method (Select "I want Amazon to ship...")

The Images Tab

Now the Images tab is probably one of the most important aspects of setting up your Product Listing. You've probably noticed in your own experience as a consumer that you are far more likely to choose to buy a product if it has a clear high-quality image on it. No one wants to buy something "sight unseen."

A great product image achieves many things, including:

- Higher click-throughs to your product page

- Higher conversions once visitors see your page

- An implied reduced risk for the consumer

You are not limited to just one image; in fact, it's better to show multiple angles of your product. You can include up to 9 images. It's best if the image has your product front and center, filling the majority of the frame against a white background. Do not add any text banners on your image— not only is it against Amazon policy, it looks chintzy to your potential customers.

You also want to use high-quality images, so make sure you use either jpg, png, or gif image file formats. You also want the resolution to be at least 1,000 pixels on one side to ensure that visitors to your product listing can utilize the zoom feature and get a really good look at your product.

The Description Tab

This is another important one. Here you will be entering a product description that reels visitors in and converts them to buyers. You have a maximum of 2000 characters in which to do this. Take advantage of Amazon's support for HTML and include some basic formatting that makes the description as easy to scan and read as possible. Go to OnlineSuccessDecoded.com and sign-up to receive the HTML template I am using. It's FREE!

As I said, I'll give you some detailed copywriting tips in the next section, but for now you can get some ideas by looking at the positive and negative reviews on competitor products. This will let you know what customers want from the product and also what they definitely DO NOT want.

You will also enter some Key Product Features on this tab. You can include a maximum of five features with 100 characters each. These are critical because they end up being one of the first things your visitors see on your Product Listing. Use this feature section to:

- Highlight features AND benefits (Sure, this blender is easy to carry but what does that mean for me?)

- Mention any guarantees you offer

- Cite a product's average rating

- Reference how rare or "fast-selling" an item is

The Keywords Tab

Here you will enter your main keyword. Make sure to include a differentiating product feature if you have room. Check on your competitors for keyword suggestions and don't forget to use Google's Keyword Planner for viable suggestions. Enter the highest ranking keyword results from the Keyword Planner in the "Search Terms" section of this tab.

Applying an Effective Copywriting Strategy

The modern marketplace is not based on actual need. If it was based on that, it wouldn't be as vibrant or lucrative. No one really needs a portable vitamin blender, but it sure does make some people feel great. That is what the modern marketplace is actually based on — making people feel good.

There are a number of motivations that compel people to buy within the general category of "feeling good". People buy items because they want to:

- Feel rich and successful

- Feel attractive

- Feel loved or sexy

- Feel safe and secure

- Feel free

- Feel healthy

- Feel like they are enjoying life and having fun

Does one of these "wants" apply to your product? It's important to have a clear understanding here of the difference between features and benefits. The features of your product are its facts: it's made of titanium, its color is silver, it's compact, and so on. Its benefits are what those features give to consumers. Titanium means it lasts a long time, so consumers won't need to replace it! Silver goes with anything and looks cool. Compact means you can carry it anywhere. You get the drift. So as you start thinking about the real benefits of your product, circle back and see whether they answer any of the above consumer motivators.

The Basic Components of Good Copy

Granted you don't have an enormous amount of space on your Product Listing page to write an opus about your product, but it is a good idea to hit some basic components as you draft your copy to give it an appealing form and to make it the kind of copy that will convert visitors into buyers. The basic outline for good copy goes something like this:

1. Headline – Summarize the product succinctly
2. Describe the problem your product fixes
3. Explain how your product fixes that problem
4. Establish your product's credibility
5. Describe the features first, then the benefits
6. Provide social proof that your product is great (Other people like this! Look at this best seller rating, etc.)

7. Describe your offer

8. Mention guarantees

9. Reference its scarcity (It won't last!)

10. Include a final Call to Action telling your consumer to pull the trigger and get in on this great deal

In short, this is how you can get the most out of the copy on your Product Listing. Make sure that you spell check and grammar check your writing. Nothing destroys confidence in a product like a misplaced apostrophe or misspelled word.

Chapter Seven - How To Get Your Products to Amazon's Fulfillment Centers

In this chapter, I want to walk you through the basics of getting your products to Amazon's fulfillment centers and managing them once they arrive. Thanks to Amazon Seller Central, you'd be amazed at how effective and user-friendly this process is.

Sending Your Products Directly to FBA

Getting your inventory to FBA involves three basic steps:

Your supplier sends the inventory directly to FBA – This bypasses the need for a third-party fulfillment company that can drive up costs and make logistics a nightmare.

Amazon supplies the shipping documents – Once you set up a Product Listing via your Seller Central account, Amazon automatically generates the shipping documents your supplier needs to get your stock to Amazon's fulfillment centers. This detailed information also lets Amazon know exactly what is in your supplier's shipment and where it needs to go at their fulfillment centers.

Your supplier sends them off via UPS – Once your supplier has the shipping documents in hand and your product packaged, all they need to do is hand it off to UPS shipping. There are also alternate shipping methods for those suppliers not within UPS's network.

How to Manage Your Inventory on Amazon

Now I want to go through the steps necessary to send off a

prepared shipment. Amazon changes the process on occasion, but as of this writing, here's how you do it:

Step 1 – From your Seller Central dashboard, click on "manage FBA inventory"

Step 2 – Select the product you want shipped from your list of products, select "Send/Replenish Inventory" and then click on "Go".

Step 3 – Review the address you are shipping the product to and make any changes if necessary. Select "case-packed products", then click on "Continue to shipping plan".

Step 4 – Enter the total number of shipment cases you are sending off, then click "Continue".

Step 5 – Skip the "Prepare Products" screen by just clicking "Continue".

Step 6 – On the next page— the Label Products screen— you can select the option of Amazon adding FNSKU stickers to your products at a cost of .20 each.

Step 7 – Select "Approve Shipments" on the Review Shipments screen. Keep in mind that Amazon may split your supplier shipment between several warehouses. This is no skin off your back— they just do this to make shipping on their end as fast and efficient as possible.

Step 8 – Select "Work on Shipment" on the next screen.

Step 9 – Enter your shipment details, including the weight and dimensions of individual product boxes, in the Prepare Shipment screen.

Step 10 – Make sure that "Small Parcel Delivery" and "Amazon Preferred Carrier – UPS" are both selected if you're sending the goods within the U.S. If you send your products from China than I recommend you to use DHL.

Step 11 – Enter the weight and dimensions of the case carrying all of your product boxes. Select Copy Last Box if you have multiple cases shipping until you reach the right number of cases.

Step 12 – Select "Calculate" to see your estimated shipping costs and then "I Agree" and "Accept Charges"

Step 13 – Finally, check off "Print Box Labels" and make sure that you save the resulting PDF to your computer.

Your first Amazon shipment is ready to go! Make sure you send everything you need to your supplier to facilitate this process. Once your supplier sends your first shipment out the door, make sure that you circle back and ensure that the shipment is "Marked as Shipped" to avoid confusion down the road. You can track your shipment via Seller Central any time and see what fulfillment center Amazon is storing it in.

If your supplier is in China, you have a slightly different process to follow. You will not be able to use UPS, Amazon's preferred carrier, and instead will have to go with DHL. DHL has a lot of information on their site about setting up shipments that will really help you work this out. The most important thing to remember is that you will need to fill out the appropriate customs way bill, and you will need to select DHL's "Delivery Duty Paid" service, which essentially allows the product to go through customs and then retroactively bills the supplier for the duty fees and taxes.

Chapter Eight - How To Launch Your Private Label Product on Amazon

You have your products ready to ship at an Amazon fulfillment center. Now how do you get attention to your brand? In this chapter, I will walk you through the steps you need to follow to launch your brand effectively on Amazon. These run the gamut from leveraging social media to utilizing promotions.

Getting 15 to 20 Reviews to Boost the Social Proof

In chapter 6, I mentioned how "social proof" is a key element of drafting good copy for your Product Page. Visitors to your page— your potential customers– want to know and *see* that other people just like them are into your product. One of the best ways to do this is through reviews.

Now, ideally having positive reviews in the 100s is a perfect scenario. Since you're just starting out, you are going to need to work hard to get that first collection of reviews for your product. You want to get at least 15 to 20 reviews in place to really give your brand the best momentum as it launches in the Amazon space. Anything in the single digits will not impress. You could get these reviews organically over time, but that may take awhile. You can remind your buyers by sending messages through Seller Central (but this is a manual process). You can automate this process by using a mailing tool like **Feedback Genius**. This tool will send custom messages to your customers after certain statuses (for example: after order confirmation, order shipment and after delivery). FG will also monitor your seller feedback and will notify you when a buyer has left negative feedback. You will receive a mail or sms.

Instead, a good idea is to turn to family and friends. Give them the product sample that you initially received from your supplier and ask them to try it out.There are a few catches you have to keep in mind:

1. You CANNOT solicit positive or fake reviews (ask for an unbiased review)

2. Your reviewers have to have been Amazon shoppers in the past

For those of you who live outside the States, your inner circle may not have spent that much time shopping on Amazon. If they have, they are good to go and they can test your product out. If they have not, you can also consider reaching out to the friends and family of U.S.-based Amazon marketplace members, appealing to them with a free trial or a deep discount on your product.

Remember, you cannot ask someone to give you a positive review. Trust in your product and ask the people involved to give you as objective a review as possible. The culture of reviews online are essential to e-commerce. What's more, most online consumers have a good "bull" detector when it comes to fake reviews, so it's not the best idea to try to pass these off.

You can also reach out to people you know through social media. Talk to your "friends" on Facebook, offering to give them a free trial in exchange for a review. Chances are you are going to get some positive ones out of this approach, as people are not typically willing to offend. Remember, your goal is 15 to 20 reviews— anything in the single digits is seen as a bad sign to the wandering and clicking consumer who makes decisions in a matter of moments. And zero reviews? A death knell for your product. So get those double digit reviews as soon as possible— ideally within a few days of posting your first product.

So go out there and see what your personal network can do for you and your growing brand on Amazon.

Launching Amazon-Sponsored Ads

Another great tool to use is the Amazon-sponsored ad. You want to get these in place AFTER you have garnered your initial group of reviews. You do not want to start driving buyer traffic to your Product Listing until it has some "buzz" around it.

Setting up your Amazon-sponsored ads is a pretty straightforward process and, most importantly, does not require a good deal of maintenance on your end. Once they are in place you can just tweak them on occasion to make sure you are getting as much out of them as possible.

Creating an Amazon Ad Campaign through Seller Central

To set up your Amazon ad campaign, head over to your Seller Central dashboard. Click on Advertising then click on "Campaign Manager". Click "Create Campaign" next and then start filling in the following information:

- Your campaign's name

- An average daily budget (start with $10 per day)

- An ad group name

- A default bid (bid more than suggested cost per click)

You will also need to select between manual targeting and automatic targeting. I recommend starting out with manual targeting. Then just select the product you want to advertise and click on "Save and Finish". Your ad should post within a matter of minutes.

Go to OnlineSuccessDecoded.com and download the step-by-step guide on how to start an Amazon sponsored ad.

Facebook Ads and AdWords

Another great option is creating a Facebook ad campaign for your product. This costs extra, of course, but if you have extra startup cash on hand, go ahead and launch a Facebook ad campaign at the same time you launch your Amazon ads. A Facebook ad campaign can be as expensiveor budget-friendly as you like, so don't worry too much.

In these early stages, Facebook ads will just drive traffic toward your product page, but in the long term as you build, you may want to consider taking advantage of Facebook ads to build a customer database, drive customers to your website, and run promotions. For now, take a look at their Self-Service Ad Creation tool; it will walk you through the basics of an FB ad campaign and help you focus your efforts in the most effective way possible.

Google AdWords

Using AdWords is a great way to drive initial traffic to your product page. The cost of a Google ad campaign can vary widely and they have different pricing structures depending on the bidding strategy you use In your campaign. A cost-per-click approach is typically the best answer for driving traffic to a site or product listing, so look into the cost of that bidding strategy and see if it works within your budget. AdWords may not be the best long-term advertising strategy for your Amazon brand, but it can help with an initial boost of traffic in these early stages.

How to Create Promotions

Everyone loves a good deal. In fact, it is one of the major motivators in a lot of the conversions that happen on Amazon. Think about how many times you have seen "FREE SHIPPING" or "30% off regular price" dangled in front of your eyes when shopping online.

There are any number of promotions in addition to the traditional shipping and discount incentives that you can use, too, all of which can engage your potential customers and help them pull the trigger on a purchase.

Setting Up an Amazon Promotion

To set up your first Amazon promotion, head into your Seller Central Account and select "Manage Promotions" from under the Advertising tab at the top of the page. On the Promotions Management page you will see four options:

- Free Shipping

- Buy One Get One Free

- Money Off, and

- External Promotions

Free Shipping is only available for products fulfilled by the merchant or FBM products. Money Off offers a discount and will be the most advantageous promotion for you. Buy One Get One Free is pretty self-explanatory, and External Promotions gives the customer some post-purchase benefit, like a discount on future purchases, for example.

For your purposes, you can't do better than the Money Off promotion, so I am going to walk you through that one right now step by step.

Setting Up a Money Off Promotion

Once you select "Money Off", you will need to create a Product Selection list. Go to "Manage Product Selections" and select "Create New Product Selection". Select your product and click on "Submit". On the next screen, create a name for your promotion or a Tracking ID. You also want to enter a description of the promotion along with the ASIN of the product. Click on "Submit".

You can also set a few conditions for the promotion.

- Set up a minimum amount in dollars the customer has to spend in order to use the promotion.
- Specify which of your products the promotion applies to
- Specify the amount of the discount, ideally using a dollar amount instead of a percentage.
- Select "Applies to Purchased Items"
- Explore the Advanced Options to add more promotion conditions such as giving a customer a discount if they buy three or more of an item

Scheduling the Promotion

Next, you'll need to schedule your promotion. It should take at least four hours for the promotion to launch. Set a start date and time if you want to launch later on along with an end date.

Additional Promotional Options

There are a few more specifics you need to set in place. One important one is selecting the Claim Code check box. This requires that any consumer who wants to take advantage of a promotion has to enter a claim code.

You also want to make sure that you select "one redemption

per customer". There are countless horror stories of poorly run promotions that resulted in customers taking advantage of such mistakes and returning again and again for a product at a deep discount. Set your limit to one per customer.

You will also see a checkbox that reads "Detail Page Display Text". Checking this means that the promotion will appear on your product page. I do not think it's a good idea to go with this option. If you are lucky enough to get some fresh eyes on your page without this promotion, you do not want them taking advantage of this discount. Click on "Review" once all of this is in place.

Proofing Your Promotion

After you click "Review", you will want to walk through your promotion and proof it in detail. If it checks out, you can click on the "Submit" button. You can always view it again after that by finding it under the "Pending" section of your promotions list.

Once your promotion posts, test it out yourself. Go through the whole process, entering the code, adding it to your cart, etc. You won't need to make the purchase, of course, but you just want to make sure that everything is in great working order.

Make sure you protect your inventory if your coupon code is leaked on Deal sites or in Facebook groups. Go to **www.OnlineSuccessDecoded.com** and sign-up to receive your FREE report on how to protect your inventory on Amazon.com.

How to Get Ranked With Your Keywords

I've let you in on a number of methods for getting traffic on your Product Listing and launching your brand effectively on

Amazon. What I have not done yet is let you in on by far one of the most effective ways to ensure a big launch for your brand— getting ranked in a top spot for your keyword.

When people go to Amazon to find an item, as you know, they enter a keyword. What happens if you are one of the first listings they see on the resulting list? Chances are they are going to click on your product. Having a spot in the Top 3 for a keyword is pretty much ideal and something that you really need to focus on to get the most momentum out of your product launch. How do you do it?

Well, you go back through everything you've learned here and make sure that all your t's are crossed and all your i's are dotted. Adhering to all my tips and tricks of the trade will put you in good stead to start moving up the keyword ranks.

You can also try to drive purchases of your product through a keyword search instead of through a direct link. As friends, family, and acquaintances start asking about your brand, do not give them a direct link. Ask them to go to Amazon.com, run a search using your product's keyword, and then *find your product on that list.*

Every time someone finds your product through a keyword search, Amazon bumps you up on the list. The more click-throughs that happen in this way that convert into purchases, the happier Amazon is with you. So, take this approach as much as possible and see what it can do for your ranking.

Chapter Nine - How To Manage Sales Tax

An important consideration every FBA seller needs to keep in mind is sales tax. Effectively managing sales tax is extremely important, as ineffective management can get you into trouble and then some. Fortunately, there are some great tools out there that can help you manage your sales tax with ease as an Amazon FBA seller.

An Introduction to Sales Tax for FBA Sellers

There is something called "nexus." Businesses with a nexus in a state have a tax liability in that state— in other words, they need to pay sales tax on their products sold in that state. The issue that comes up with FBA that a good number of people do not realize is that with Amazon FBA, you have the responsibility for not one state but *multi-state tax compliance.*

Why? Because the FBA fulfillment centers are located all over the place, in states across the U.S. The inventory you have stored in each of these fulfillment centers serves as "nexus", establishing your business as a tax-liable entity in that state.

Sound intimidating? Not especially. There are tools in place, including a great website called Taxjar.com that can help you organize and manage multi-state tax compliance.

Which Software to Use to Track Your Sales Tax

As mentioned, TaxJar is one of the best options for managing your multi-state tax compliance for selling through Amazon FBA. Start off with their helpful State Sales Tax Map. You can click on individual states and get detailed information on that state's sales tax requirements. *Very detailed,* including every-thing from sales tax rates to how to charge your customers and the tax rules related to shipping and handling. Each state page will also give you information on the registration requirements for your business within that state.

More good news is that TaxJar offers support specifically for multi-channel state situations like Amazon FBA. They'll organize your sales tax data and help you manage things quite efficiently. They also have an AutoFile feature that automatically files your sales tax in each state for you, so you don't need to stress deadlines.

They have several plans that you can choose to sign up with that run from a Basic plan at $8.95 per month to a Premier plan that charges $89.95 per month. Since these are based on how many sales transactions you have each month and how often you rely on the TaxJar interface, you may be okay starting out with a Basic package.

You will want to scale up as your business grows to make sure you are keeping up with your Amazon FBA sales tax obligation as your brand expands.

Disclaimer: I am not a tax specialist or licensed tax attorney. The information provided here should be used as a general guide. For specific questions about your own taxes, please consult a tax specialist or refer to the official IRS publications.

Conclusion

This book "Amazon FBA Decoded" is the only book that shows you every step to go from "no idea" to your first $15,000. You can choose if you want an (offline) small business that generates a few thousand dollars a month...or if you want to go "all in" and build a semi-automated business to generate income streams of 5 figures, 6 figures, even 7 figures a year, passively. Either way, your Amazon FBA business is like a steady companion who "works" even as you sleep.

If you've always wanted to start an online business -- to take your passion and share it with the world in a way that lets you craft your dream lifestyle -- this book can show you how.

It's natural to have questions if you're about to make a big step, but believe me starting an Amazon FBA business is definitely worth it.The question is if you are going to change your current situation and if you are going to take action!

Do you really want to be financially free and work when you want and where you want?

- You will have **more time for yourself and your family**. You will work only 10 hours per week.

- You will **make more money**: earnings from $15k to 100k per month are achievable.

- You are building a **"real business"** and creating a brand that's worth capital. When you want you can sell your business.

So, what are you waiting for?

Take action and live the life you desire and pursue your passions.

If you have a 9 to 5 corporate job, you can still start your Amazon FBA business by working part-time (2 hours per day). Within a year you can quit your job and focus on your Amazon business.

I know that there are many other passive income options in the market. I have done them all (selling ebooks, affiliate marketing, drop shipping, ...)

The Amazon FBA business is a lot more fun to work than all the other online opportunities.

I hope this book will change your life or will trigger you to think about the rest of your life.

If you have any questions just visit my website **OnlineSuccessDecoded.com** and contact me.

I will be glad to help in any way I can.

Oh, if you enjoyed this book, please take the time to share your thoughts and post a review on Amazon. It would be greatly appreciated!

To your success,

Erdal Gul

www.ingramcontent.com/pod-product-compliance
Lightning Source LLC
Chambersburg PA
CBHW070917180526
45168CB00005B/2044